FOREST
ECOSYSTEMS

by Tammy Gagne

www.12StoryLibrary.com

12-Story Library is an imprint of Bookstaves and Press Room Editions

Produced for 12-Story Library by Red Line Editorial

Photographs ©: Ryan Tanguilan/Shutterstock Images, cover, 1; AustralianCamera/Shutterstock Images, 4; StillFX/Shutterstock Images, 5; LMspencer/Shutterstock Images, 6; alybaba/Shutterstock Images, 7; Peerapong Pongtonglo/Shutterstock Images, 8; jannoon028/Shutterstock Images, 9; feathercollector/ Shutterstock Images, 10; Ben Queenborough/Shutterstock Images, 11; Nancy Kennedy/Shutterstock Images, 12; KMNPhoto/Shutterstock Images, 13; Wildnerdpix/Shutterstock Images, 14; Svetlana Bondareva/Shutterstock Images, 15; Dave Allen Photography/Shutterstock Images, 16; Pim Leijen/ Shutterstock Images, 17, 28 (bottom); lexan/Shutterstock Images, 18; Pi-Lens/Shutterstock Images, 19, 20; Brian Lasenby/Shutterstock Images, 21; G Seeger/Shutterstock Images, 22; Dennis van de Water/Shutterstock Images, 23; B Brown/Shutterstock Images, 24; JHVEPhoto/Shutterstock Images, 25; bikeriderlondon/Shutterstock Images, 26; Robert Crum/Shutterstock Images, 27; critterbiz/ Shutterstock Images, 28 (top); Ricardo Reitmeyer/Shutterstock Images, 28 (middle); chris froome/ Shutterstock Images, 29 (top left); vesilvio/Shutterstock Images, 29 (bottom left); Oleksandrum/ Shutterstock Images, 29 (top right); Chris Hill/Shutterstock Images, 29 (bottom right)

Content Consultant: Lucy Kerhoulas, Assistant Professor, Forest Ecophysiology, Humboldt State University

Library of Congress Cataloging-in-Publication Data
Names: Gagne, Tammy.
Title: Forest ecosystems / by Tammy Gagne.
Description: Mankato, MN : 12 Story Library, [2018] | Series: Earth's
    ecosystem | Audience: Grade 4 to 6. | Includes bibliographical references
    and index.
Identifiers: LCCN 2016047141 (print) | LCCN 2016047753 (ebook) | ISBN
    9781632354556 (hardcover : alk. paper) | ISBN 9781632355218 (pbk. : alk.
    paper) | ISBN 9781621435730 (hosted e-book)
Subjects: LCSH: Forest ecology--Juvenile literature.
Classification: LCC QH541.5.F6 G3425 2018 (print) | LCC QH541.5.F6 (ebook) |
    DDC 577.3--dc23
LC record available at https://lccn.loc.gov/2016047141

Printed in China
022017

Access free, up-to-date content on this topic plus a full digital version of this book. Scan the QR code on page 31 or use your school's login at 12StoryLibrary.com.

Table of Contents

Tropical Evergreen Forests Contain Many Species 4

The Congo Rainforest Is Thriving in Central Africa 6

Tropical Deciduous Forests Are Rare Ecosystems 8

Many Animals Live in Forests 10

Many Temperate Evergreen Trees Produce Cones 12

The Redwood Forest Is a Temperate Rain Forest 14

Temperate Deciduous Forests Get Rainfall All Year 16

Boreal Forests Are Harsh Environments 18

Canada's Boreal Forest Is Vast 20

Forest Plants Include Trees and More 22

People Are Harming Forest Ecosystems 24

People Can Help Care for Forest Ecosystems 26

Deciduous Forest Food Web 28

Glossary 30

For More Information 31

Index 32

About the Author 32

Tropical Evergreen Forests Contain Many Species

Forests are made up of many living things. Groups of living things and their environment are called ecosystems. Forest ecosystems are found on every continent of the world, except Antarctica. Within each forest ecosystem are other ecosystems.

Hundreds of woody plant species make up the world's tropical evergreen forests. Also known as tropical rain forests, these warm and wet ecosystems are some of the most important in the world. They help maintain the climate across the globe. They are also home to some of the rarest animal and plant species on the planet.

As their name suggests, evergreen trees are always green. They keep their leaves all year long. Rain forests are always growing. As some

Some of the most valuable medications come from plants found in tropical rain forests.

A tropical rain forest has everything it needs for survival right within its ecosystem.

plants die, other trees and plants use them as nutrients.

The tallest trees in tropical rain forests can reach heights of 292 feet (89 m). They thrive from the regular rainfall and sunlight. Just below them are trees that do better in the shade. These trees can still grow as high as 79 to 118 feet (24 to 36 m). The ground in tropical rain forest ecosystems is covered with vegetation. It includes ferns and mosses. These plants need almost no sunlight.

75

Amount of rain, in inches (191 cm), a forest must get each year to be called a rain forest.

- Tropical evergreen forests, or tropical rain forests, contain hundreds of woody plant species.
- Trees in these ecosystems can grow up to 292 feet (89 m) tall.
- Trees and plants in tropical rain forests use materials from decaying plants as nutrients.
- Tropical rain forest plants near the ground can thrive with little to no sunlight.

THINK ABOUT IT

Based on the information you have read here, why do you think rain forests are always growing? Give evidence to support your answer.

The Congo Rainforest Is Thriving in Central Africa

The second-largest rain forest in the world is in central Africa. The Congo Rainforest is a tropical evergreen forest found mainly in the Democratic Republic of the Congo. The forest also stretches into several other countries. Only the Amazon Rainforest is larger.

The Congo Rainforest is home to thousands of animal species. About 1,000 of these species are birds. Another 700 are fish. Many small mammals,

The Congo Rainforest is known for having gorillas.

UNESCO SITES

The United Nations Educational, Scientific, and Cultural Organization (UNESCO) has made a list of places that have "outstanding universal value" to the world. Called World Heritage sites, these places include natural resources and man-made landmarks. UNESCO has granted this honor to five national parks within the Congo Rainforest.

such as red-tailed monkeys and chimpanzees, make their homes in the tallest trees. Larger animals, such as elephants and gorillas, rely on trees for food. These herbivores help shape the forest ecosystem by eating smaller trees. This keeps the trees from taking over the forests.

More than 11,000 plant species grow in the rain forests of the Democratic Republic of the Congo. About 1,100 of these species are found nowhere else on Earth.

Deforestation has become one of the biggest threats to the world's forests. Trees are often cut down to make room for farming or buildings. When this happens, numerous species of animals and plants become threatened. Since 1990, the Congo Rainforest has suffered the least amount of deforestation of all the world's major forests.

440 million

Number of acres (178 million ha) the Congo Rainforest takes up in central Africa.

- The Congo Rainforest is the second-largest tropical evergreen forest in the world.
- The forest spans several different countries, with most of it lying in the Democratic Republic of the Congo.
- The Congo Rainforest contains more than 10,000 animal species.

Bauhinia galpinii is a type of shrub that grows in the Congo Rainforest.

3

Tropical Deciduous Forests Are Rare Ecosystems

While evergreen trees keep their leaves all year, deciduous trees do not. These trees drop their leaves each year. They grow new ones later. Most deciduous forests are found in parts of the world with four distinct seasons. But tropical deciduous forests stay warm all or most of the year. These ecosystems are also called monsoon forests. They are most common in Southeast Asia.

Trees in tropical deciduous forest ecosystems lose their leaves during the dry season. Without enough water, the leaves die. The trees drop their leaves in order to survive. When

100

Height, in feet (30 m), of many trees growing in a tropical deciduous forest.

- Trees in tropical deciduous forests drop their leaves during the dry season each year.
- These ecosystems are also called monsoon forests.
- New leaves start growing at the beginning of the rainy season.
- Teak, sandalwood, and bamboo all grow in tropical deciduous forests.

Orchids are often found in monsoon forests.

8

there is more rain, the trees grow new leaves.

Tropical deciduous forests have many unique trees and woody plants. Teak, sandalwood, and bamboo all grow in monsoon forests. These types of wood are very important to many people in India. They make their livings harvesting them.

Bamboo is common in tropical deciduous forests.

Many Animals Live in Forests

Forests ecosystems have a wide variety of animal species. They provide an ideal home for many creatures, large and small. Brown bears can grow up to 6 feet (1.8 m) tall. They can weigh up to 800 pounds (363 kg). The red cockaded woodpecker is not nearly as big. This bird species is just 8.5 inches (22 cm) long. It weighs about 1.5 ounces (43 g).

Each forest animal plays a role within its ecosystem. Predators, such as wolves, help keep the

The red cockaded woodpecker has a wingspan of 15 inches (38 cm).

55 to 130

Average weight, in pounds (25 to 59 kg), of the gray wolf.

- Forests contain many different animal species.
- From bears to birds, these animals range in size greatly.
- Predators help forest ecosystems by keeping the populations of their prey from rising too much.
- Deforestation and pollution are harming endangered animal species.

populations of other animals from increasing too much. The Amazon Rainforest's black agouti eats fruits and nuts that have fallen to the forest floor. These rodents often hide Brazil nuts to dig up later. When agoutis forget to do so, the nuts can grow into new Brazil nut trees.

The future is uncertain for many forest animals. The red Uakari monkey, the northern spotted owl, and the pygmy elephant are just a few endangered species.

JUST ONE JAGUAR LEFT

One of the most endangered forest animals is the jaguar. Over the past century, these large cats have almost entirely disappeared from the United States. In 2016, the last-known wild jaguar in the country was caught on video in Arizona. Without a mate, this jaguar is likely to be the last of its kind in this region of North America.

Problems such as deforestation and pollution threaten these species and many others.

Many Temperate Evergreen Trees Produce Cones

Most temperate evergreen forests are found in areas with warm summers and cold winters. Some have mostly needleleaf trees, such as spruce trees. Others are largely made up of trees with broad leaves, such as magnolia trees.

Magnolia trees are known for their big, beautiful flowers.

22.9
Length, in inches (58 cm), of the longest pine cone on record.

- Temperate evergreen trees generally grow in places with warm, dry summers and cold, wet winters.
- Some temperate evergreens have needles, while others have broad leaves.
- Needleleaf trees, or coniferous trees, produce cones instead of flowers.
- All evergreens lose their needles or leaves, but new growth happens all the time.

Conifers reproduce with seed and pollen cones.

Needleleaf evergreens are also called coniferous trees. This is because they produce cones instead of flowers. One of the best-known coniferous trees is the pine. Many people use pinecones in craft projects or for decorating. Because pine trees grow fast and straight, pine is a popular building material.

Although evergreens always have leaves or needles, this does not mean they do not drop any. Evergreens are in a constant state of growth. Old needles fall out as new ones grow in their place.

THINK ABOUT IT

Based on what you have read here, do you think spruce trees ever drop their needles? Give evidence to support your answer.

13

The Redwood Forest Is a Temperate Rain Forest

The Redwood Forest is a special kind of temperate evergreen forest. It is found in northern California and southern Oregon. This forest contains the tallest tree species in the world. The tallest redwood tree is 379 feet (116 m) high.

The Redwood Forest is not located in the tropics. The temperature stays mostly between 45 and 60 degrees Fahrenheit (7.2 and 16˚C) regardless of the season. But the Redwood Forest is considered a rain forest. The area gets between 60 and 80 inches (152 and 203 cm) of rain each year.

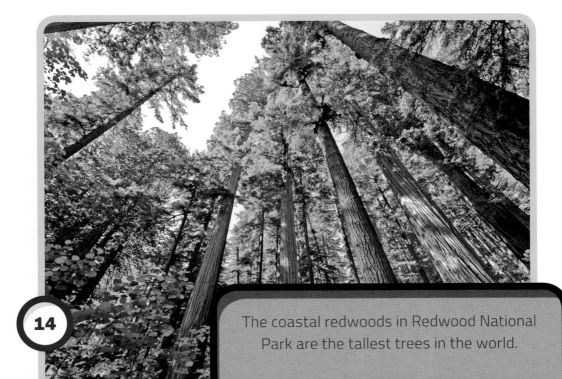

The coastal redwoods in Redwood National Park are the tallest trees in the world.

Redwood trees are only one of the many types of plants found in the Redwood Forest. Underneath these massive evergreens are smaller trees, shrubs, and other plants. Azaleas, rhododendrons, and sword ferns are some of the most common plant species.

Temperate rain forests are filled with many animals. Black-tailed deer, bobcats, and raccoons all live in the Redwood Forest. The creeks within this forest are full of life. They contain species such as salmon and trout.

2,200
Age, in years, of the oldest coastal redwood tree.

- Redwoods are the tallest trees in the world.
- The Redwood Forest is a rain forest, even though it is not in the tropics.
- The Redwood Forest gets up to 80 inches (203 cm) of rain each year.
- The forest contains many plant and animal species.

Temperate Deciduous Forests Get Rainfall All Year

Temperate deciduous forests are always changing. These ecosystems do not have a rainy season and a dry season. Instead, they have four seasons, with precipitation year-round. But the changing temperatures cause the trees to drop their leaves.

As spring starts, trees in temperate deciduous forests begin to bud. Leaves are fully formed before the start of summer. As cooler temperatures arrive in autumn,

Hardwood trees, such as oaks, are common in temperate deciduous forests.

The red fox is one type of mammal found in temperate deciduous forests.

leaves change color and fall to the ground. Trees go through a dormant period in winter, when they remain bare. The process starts over each year.

Animals living in a temperate deciduous forest must change with the seasons. Some, such as the black bear, hibernate during winter. Many birds migrate to warmer regions when the air turns cold. Some, including the American bald eagle, may stay for the winter. But if food becomes scarce, this species will fly south.

200,000
Number of leaves on the average adult deciduous tree.

- Temperate deciduous forests receive precipitation during every season.
- Trees in these ecosystems grow leaves in spring and drop them during fall.
- The trees remain leafless throughout winter.
- Animals living in these forests adapt or leave the forest when colder weather arrives.

Boreal Forests Are Harsh Environments

The boreal forest lies just south of the tundra in Asia, Europe, and North America. It does not get as cold as the tundra. But it is still a harsh environment. In addition to trees, the boreal forest ecosystem has thousands of lakes, rivers, and wetlands.

Only hardy species can survive in the boreal forest. This means there are fewer animal and plant species in the boreal forest than in deciduous or tropical forests.

THINK ABOUT IT

Animal species deal with living in the boreal forest in different ways. How might they cope with the colder weather? How might larger animals, such as bears, survive the winter weather when food becomes scarce?

The boreal forest is also called taiga, which means "forest" in Russian.

12,000

Number of years since the boreal forest was covered by glaciers.

- Boreal forest ecosystems are found on the continents of Asia, Europe, and North America.
- Fewer animal and plant species live in the boreal forest than in warmer forest ecosystems.
- The shape and spacing of the trees in the boreal forest help them survive the harsh conditions of this ecosystem.

Most of the plants in the boreal forest are coniferous trees. Pine, white spruce, and balsam fir trees are some of the most common. A waxy coating called the cuticle helps protect conifer leaves from freezing temperatures. The wax also holds in moisture so the trees can survive dry periods when soil water is frozen.

Trees in the boreal forest grow close to one another. This shields them from the wind and snow. The shape of boreal forest evergreens is useful in the cold climate. The top branches are shorter, with wider ones near the bottom. The trees grow slanted so that heavy snow falls off the branches instead of breaking them.

The boreal forest is named after the Greek god of the north wind, Boreas.

Canada's Boreal Forest Is Vast

More than half of Canada's land is made up of boreal forest. This large ecosystem is home to more than 2.5 million people. It is a key part of the country's natural environment and economy.

Many Canadians depend on the boreal forest

for their livelihoods. Some people harvest trees. Others make wood and paper products from the trees that are cut down. Some people plant new trees to replace the ones harvested in this region.

The boreal forest supports a wide variety of wildlife,

The boreal forest of Canada's Yukon territory in the winter

30

Number of boreal forest bird species that remain in the forest throughout the winter.

- More than 2.5 million people live in Canada's boreal forest.
- Many of these people work in the forests.
- A wide range of animal species inhabit this ecosystem.
- More than 200 of Canada's bird species live in the boreal forest.

despite its cold temperatures. Black bears, caribou, and moose are among the largest mammals found in the area. Smaller animals, such as beavers and muskrats, also live in the boreal forest. All these species have thick coats to keep them warm year-round.

Birds are common in the boreal forest region. Half of Canada's 425 bird species live here. Some of the best-known species include the Canada goose and the great blue heron. Both species fly south during the coldest times of the year.

SPECIAL SEALS

Canada's boreal forest is home to a rare animal. Most seals live in salt water. But Lacs des Loups Marins harbor seals swim in the lakes and rivers of northern Quebec. This is the only place in the world they are found. This seal species lived in the ocean between 3,000 and 8,000 years ago. As ice from the Ice Age melted into the world's oceans and rivers, some marine species became landlocked. Lacs des Loups Marins harbor seals were among them. About 300 of these seals remain. They are now part of the boreal forest ecosystem.

Forest Plants Include Trees and More

Forests have several layers of plant life. The top layer is often called the canopy. Here, the treetops grow toward the sun. The canopy prevents too much sun from reaching the plant life below. Many plants grow best with only a small amount of sun.

The understory is located below the canopy. This layer is made up of smaller trees. They may grow to about 65 feet (20 m) tall. They have thinner trunks than the larger trees of the canopy.

The petrified trees at Petrified Forest National Park are no longer alive.

PETRIFIED FOREST NATIONAL PARK

The Petrified Forest National Park is located in northern Arizona. About 200 million years ago, many trees in this region were buried by an ancient river. The trees absorbed minerals and other sediments in the water. Over time, the trees hardened into a stony substance that is more like rock than wood. The national park also has many living trees and other plant life. It is well known for its colorful wildflowers that bloom each summer.

El Yunque National Forest is located in Puerto Rico.

The third layer is just below the understory. It is called the shrub layer. It is made up of small woody plants. Shrubs can grow to about 10 feet (3 m) tall. The shrub layer also contains young trees that will become understory or canopy trees as adults.

The two bottom layers of the forest are the herbaceous layer and the forest floor. The herbaceous layer is made up of ferns, grasses, and flowering plants. The forest floor contains all the dead matter that falls from the other plant life within the ecosystem. Fallen leaves and cones become food for the other plant life in the forest. Branches from fallen trees often contain water. This moisture can help seedlings grow. Plants such as mosses, liverworts, mushrooms, and lichens also live on the forest floor.

6,000
Weight, in pounds (2,722 kg), of oxygen that a tree can produce in its lifetime.

- The canopy and understory are where most trees grow.
- The shrub layer contains woody plants and younger trees.
- All plants in the forest ecosystem benefit from the nutrients released into the soil of the forest floor.

People Are Harming Forest Ecosystems

People affect the world's forests each day. One of the biggest ways they do this is by cutting down trees. People use wood to build houses, businesses, and furniture. As the world's population rises, the need for wood also grows. Problems arise when older trees are cut down faster than new trees can grow to replace them.

In many parts of the world, growing populations mean people are taking up more land from forests. New trees cannot grow where houses now stand or where food is being farmed. There is a higher demand for wood and less forest to take the wood from.

The wood from many tree species makes excellent building materials.

58,000

Area, in square miles (150,219 sq km), of forest that is lost each year due to clear-cutting and other factors.

- People can hurt forest ecosystems by cutting down too many trees too quickly.
- Building homes and farms on forest land is another way people can harm this ecosystem.
- Once land is used for homes or farms, it is unlikely to return to forest land.
- Many animal and plant species become endangered as more trees are cut down.

As many as one billion monarchs migrate from Canada to Mexico each year.

Once people begin living or farming on the land, the forest has almost no chance of returning.

Clear-cutting impacts more than just trees. Animals and other plants also suffer. Monarch butterflies migrate south from Canada and the northeastern United States each year. Many of them spend their winters thousands of miles away in coniferous forests in Mexico. Due to deforestation, there are fewer trees in Mexico. This has threatened monarch butterflies. Many other animals face similar threats.

People Can Help Care for Forest Ecosystems

Like animals and plants, people depend on forest ecosystems. One of the most important things forests do is store carbon dioxide. When there is more carbon dioxide in the air, temperatures rise. This causes global warming. The more carbon dioxide that stays in forests, the less it adds to global warming.

Conservation can help forest ecosystems. Large organizations, such as the Nature Conservancy and the World Wildlife Fund, work to preserve the world's forests. People can help by volunteering or giving money to conservation groups.

WORKING TOGETHER IN TEXAS

The golden-cheeked warbler nests only in Texas. A group of ranchers in Texas has partnered with the US Army to protect this bird. The ranchers rent part of their land to the army. It is left unused. Today, about 5,000 pairs of golden-cheeked warblers live in the forests near the Fort Hood army base. This is about half of the species' total population.

Recycling can help keep forests healthy.

recycle

Making good choices is an important step in caring for the world's forests. Reusing wood to build things helps reduce the number of trees that need to be cut down. When people must use new wood, they can choose species that grow quickly. Douglas fir trees are a good choice.

It might seem like one person cannot make a difference. But that one person can share knowledge with others about why forest ecosystems are important to the world. By recycling and using less paper, people can reduce the number of trees cut down each day. Together, everyone can help save the forests and the many species within them.

5.57

Average number of trees per year used to make paper products for each person in the United States.

- Volunteering for or donating to conservation groups is one way to help protect the forests.
- It is important to make responsible decisions when using wood.
- Recycling wood instead of using new materials helps reduce the number of trees that need to be cut down.
- Sharing knowledge about the importance of forest ecosystems can help save them.

Deciduous Forest Food Web

black bear

white-tailed deer

red fox

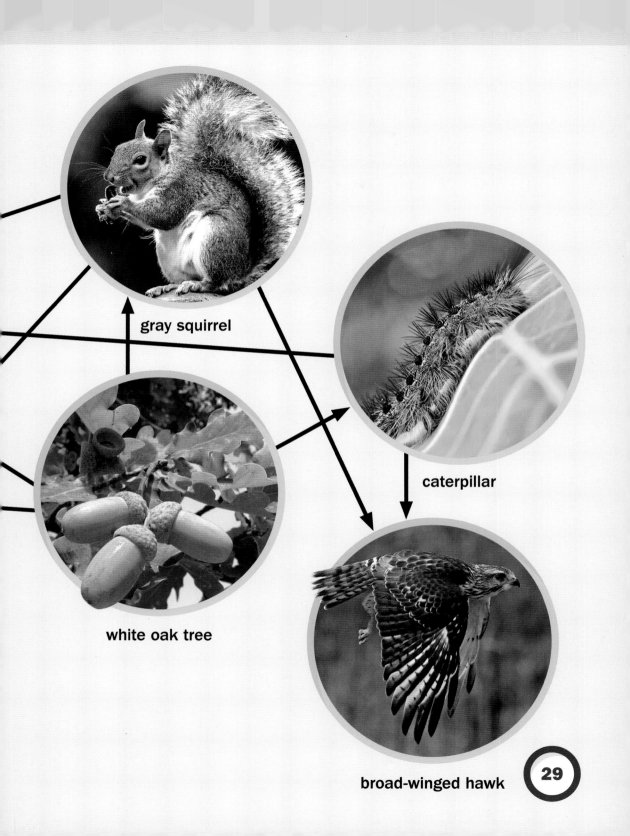

gray squirrel

caterpillar

white oak tree

broad-winged hawk

Glossary

clear-cutting
The act of cutting down a large area of trees all at once.

climate
The weather in a particular place.

conservation
The act of protecting a natural resource.

deforestation
The clearing of trees from land.

dormant
To slow down or become inactive for a period of time.

herbivores
Animals that eat plants only.

hibernate
To pass the winter in a restful state.

migrate
To move from one region to another, often due to the changing seasons.

nutrients
Substances a living thing uses for survival and growth.

precipitation
Water that falls to the ground as snow or rain.

predators
Animals that hunt other animals for food.

tundra
A large Arctic region found in parts of Europe, Asia, and North America in which the subsoil is permanently frozen and there are no trees.

For More Information

Books

Gagne, Tammy. *Jaguars*. Mankato, MN: Capstone Press, 2012.

Montgomery, Sy. *Amazon Adventure: How Tiny Fish Are Saving the World's Largest Rainforest*. Boston: Houghton Mifflin Harcourt, 2017.

Pettiford, Rebecca. *Forest Food Chains*. Minneapolis, MN: Jump!, 2017.

Visit 12StoryLibrary.com

Scan the code or use your school's login at **12StoryLibrary.com** for recent updates about this topic and a full digital version of this book. Enjoy free access to:

- Digital ebook
- Breaking news updates
- Live content feeds
- Videos, interactive maps, and graphics
- Additional web resources

Note to educators: Visit 12StoryLibrary.com/register to sign up for free premium website access. Enjoy live content plus a full digital version of every 12-Story Library book you own for every student at your school.

Index

Asia, 18

bamboo, 9
bears, 10, 17, 21
beavers, 21
birds, 6, 10, 17, 21
butterflies, 25

canopy, 22–23
clear-cutting, 25
coniferous, 13, 19, 25
conservation, 26

deciduous, 8–9, 16–17, 18
deforestation, 7, 11, 25
Democratic Republic of the Congo, 6–7

elephants, 7, 11
Europe, 18
evergreen trees, 4, 6, 8, 12–13, 14–15

fish, 6–7
forest floor, 11, 23

global warming, 26
gorillas, 7

Mexico, 25
monsoon forests, 8–9

North America, 18

Petrified Forest National Park, 22
pinecones, 13
precipitation, 16
predators, 10

Redwood Forest, 14–15

shrubs, 15, 23
Southeast Asia, 8

understory, 22–23
United States, 25

wolves, 10
wood, 20, 24, 27
woodpeckers, 10
woody plants, 4, 9, 23

About the Author

Tammy Gagne has written more than 150 books for adults and children. She resides in northern New England with her husband and son. One of her favorite pastimes is visiting schools to talk to kids about the writing process.